The Ant

by Betsy Samuels

Harcourt
SCHOOL PUBLISHERS

Cover Photolibrary.com; 3 ©Dawn M. Turner/Morgue File; 4–5 ©Harcourt Education/Lewis Chandler; 6 ©Harcourt Education/Dimitrios Prokopis; 7 ©Photolibrary.com; 8 ©APL/Minden Pictures; 9–12 ©Photolibrary.com; 13 ©Auscape; 14 ©Nature Picture Library/Premaphotos

Copyright © by Harcourt, Inc.

All rights reserved. No part of this publication may be reproduced or transmitted in any form or by any means, electronic or mechanical, including photocopy, recording, or any information storage and retrieval system, without permission in writing from the publisher.

Requests for permission to make copies of any part of the work should be addressed to School Permissions and Copyrights, Harcourt, Inc., 6277 Sea Harbor Drive, Orlando, Florida 32887-6777. Fax: 407-345-2418.

HARCOURT and the Harcourt Logo are trademarks of Harcourt, Inc., registered in the United States of America and/or other jurisdictions.

Printed in China

ISBN 10: 0-15-350656-3
ISBN 13: 978-0-15-350656-7

Ordering Options
ISBN 10: 0-15-350599-0 (Grade 2 On-Level Collection)
ISBN 13: 978-0-15-350599-7 (Grade 2 On-Level Collection)
ISBN 10: 0-15-357837-8 (package of 5)
ISBN 13: 978-0-15-357837-3 (package of 5)

If you have received these materials as examination copies free of charge, Harcourt School Publishers retains title to the materials and they may not be resold. Resale of examination copies is strictly prohibited and is illegal.

Possession of this publication in print format does not entitle users to convert this publication, or any portion of it, into electronic format.

4 5 6 7 8 9 10   985   15 14 13 12 11 10 09 08

An Ant Nest

This hole leads into an ant nest. Lots of ants live together in a nest. There are many tunnels and chambers in the nest.

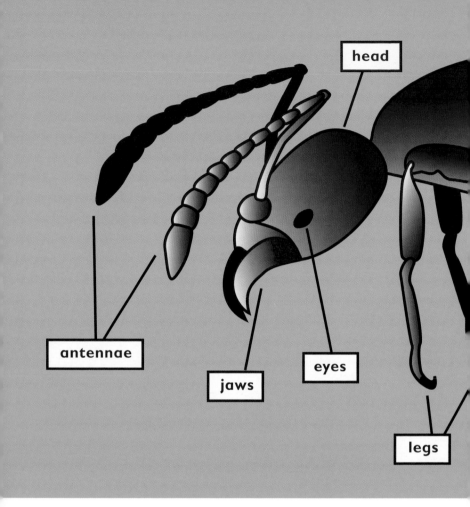

head

antennae

jaws

eyes

legs

Parts of an Ant

Ants are insects. All insects have six legs and three parts to their bodies—the head, the thorax, and the abdomen.

4

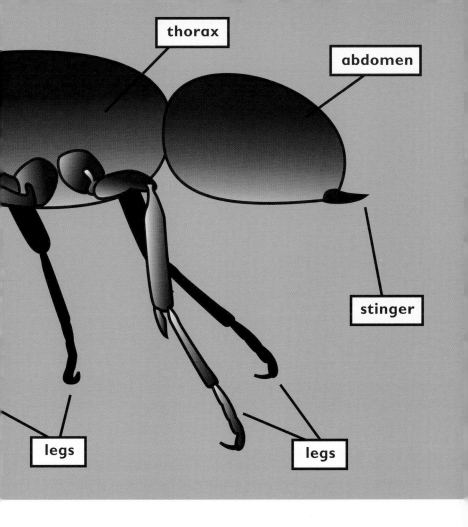

Some ants have a stinger. They all have two antennae.

There are thousands of different types of ants.

Ant Colonies

The group of ants living in a nest is called a colony. The ants in the colony work together.

The ants that look after the nest are called worker ants. Worker ants are female ants that don't lay eggs.

Worker Ants

Each worker ant has a job. Some look after the eggs. Some make the nest bigger. Some collect food, such as fruit and insects, to feed the colony. Some defend the nest and attack enemies, such as other insects and bigger animals.

egg

The Queen Ant

Each colony has a queen ant. A queen ant is bigger than a worker ant.

Only the queen ant can lay eggs. She lays many eggs. The eggs are tiny.

Ant Larvae

When the eggs hatch, larvae come out.
Ant larvae look like little worms. They eat
food brought to them by worker ants. As
the larvae get bigger, they shed their skin.

Spinning Cocoons

Soon, the larvae spin cocoons around themselves. They change into ants inside the cocoons. When the ants come out of their cocoons, they are adult ants. It usually takes six to ten weeks for an ant to develop into an adult from the time the egg is laid.

Leaving the Nest

When the queen lays her first batches of eggs, they are worker ants. The queen is building up the colony. When the colony is big enough, the queen lays more eggs. The ants from these eggs are queens and males. Worker ants stay in the nest. The male and queen ants disappear from the nest to mate.

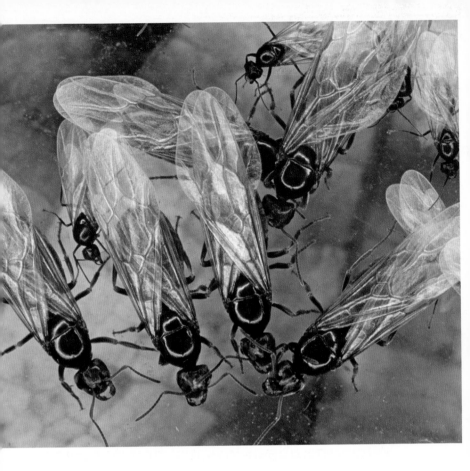

The male ants and queen ants have wings. They crowd together and pursue mates while they are flying. Soon after mating, the male ants die. Each queen ant finds somewhere safe to lay her eggs. This becomes a new nest.

A New Nest

When the queen ant is carefully sealed
inside her new nest, she sheds her wings.
Then she lays her eggs. She looks after the
eggs and larvae. When the new ants come
out of the cocoons, they are all worker
ants. They take over the job of looking
after the new eggs and larvae.

A New Colony

When the colony is big enough, the queen ant lays more eggs. These eggs become male and queen ants. The new males will fly away to mate with queen ants, and new nests are started.

The pattern of life starts all over again.

Think Critically

1. What is the name given to a group of ants that live in a nest?

2. Read pages 9 and 10 again. List the stages that ant larvae go through as they grow into adult ants.

3. Look at the diagram on pages 4–5. What are the three main parts of an ant's body called?

4. Which kind of ant do you think is the most important in the colony? Why?

5. What kind of ant in a colony would you like to be?

 Science

Create a Dictionary Create your own dictionary of ant words from the book. Write the word and what it means.

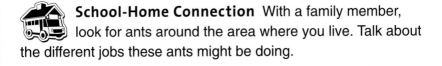 **School-Home Connection** With a family member, look for ants around the area where you live. Talk about the different jobs these ants might be doing.

Word Count: 476 (487 with words in graphics)